Anne Waldman & Pamela Lawton

Sweet-Voiced [Mutilated] Papyrus

for George Schneeman

Spuyten Duyvil
New York City

The Author and Artist would like thank Jacqueline Terrassa and Michelle Hagewood of the Metropolitan Museum of Art for facilitating our collaboration in a public forum at the museum. The Greek and Roman and Southeast Asian galleries were a third collaborator in the exploration and inspiration for this work.

Copyright ©2016 Anne Waldman
Images copyright ©2016 Pamela Lawton
ISBN 978-1-941550-49-6

Library of Congress Cataloging-in-Publication Data

Waldman, Anne, 1945-
[Poems. Selections]
Sweet-voiced [mutilated] papyrus / Anne Waldman ; Pamela Lawton.
pages ; cm
ISBN 978-1-941550-49-6
I. Lawton, Pamela. II. Title.
PS3573.A4215A6 2015
811'.54--dc23
2015006949

SKULL

he -- his sex…………………………..
   no doubt
  & violence of urbanity

or in fields of asphodel comes the risk

/////////////////////////////////

comes with some stronger rivers
       out of a swallow's song
in Africa   mixing it up

his blade   wilde beesties

ageless leader kneels in humility
   slays peacocks in the garden

 without roses
no leisure to stack on a pedestal
       for a wrestling competition in Mytilene, eh?
or as child reads warming of his future planet

she was wont to "go choral"

she – an elegant couplet with bladed axe headgear

[ ][ ][ ][ ][ ]

Phaeon! Phaeon! to cry in entourage
& follow him as a camp follower   must   secretly

or not so   gives traction to the other side

enter the horserace
as a stallion fragments   or it might kill you

---

skull: *propitious, as you mark time, homunculus*
foot: *scansion never deprives you of a way to walk out*
waist: *measure the girth of...call it philosophy? frag...*

stupid heart: don't die for love or politics

Stupid Heart

love you, I said, not the terrible word "frag"
if you follow the advice a witch gives you
you will be the best head-of-state

if you charge yourself over a cliff and drown you'll be
but one fool coiffed in suicide

emblem of yourself as figment   as the radiant Sappho is

don't forget to complain   was she bitter? jealous?

Hermes Trismegistis is a bizarre companion

if you want your magic straight he's a good old phenomenon

it's his blade to tell of "wilde beesties" of meanads

a prince   dusty philology you say.... relic of a pal
"get on stage", you're in Rome

abjure all media control while you win

& with a voice like sandpaper, ratchet it up, poet
keep dancing

if you croak they will cast your bones with the heathens

---

stupid heart: *don't die for love or politics*
thigh: *last shape, sigh or scythe*
ankle: *sexy, with ringlet component*

Eyes

ringtone a true lyre as Sappho is
I come to you with armadas puffing smoke
deserve better than classified droning, insects of late fall
& stake in electoral politics and their new judges

the hills are turning red
ochre of the amphora

eyes work their way up the charts
long gone "over there", the bed's made again
in a passion of wild thought-forms......................[[]]

the hills are turning blue

to capture a city is a crime a whole enemy
provides the validity of   testament for
lost cause, a first strike. Relic of a pal

....

sudden rifts of disaster and disclosure
secret memos to the blabber
flames abut the heart
it's not a real city actually
but one you made up hoping there is at least one last "republic" left
with memorials and towers
when there are no borders anymore

―――――――――――――――――――――――――――――

eyes: *scan the horizon for unfriendly ships*
elbow: *bends as a will does, and manly too*
thumb: *not particularly opposed*

Ears

borders?
perfect for the prefecture not an endgame
birds fall like stones from the sky
what was aviary or constellation

this is Troy, this is the she I spoke of....
It's the year of the wooden horse

turn into powder so you escape

twine yourself, twin yourself, lawgiver
contradictions cannot be true at the same time

study the map study the tricks of embattlement
my poetry comes from passion
& I am the messenger of a shaken hostess
working poison out of her blood
so, urban barbarian
don't be so fucking proud: "I get it"

---

ears: *melody or scandal*
les ongles: *scratch*
tendon: *one more memory in the system*

Brunette

obey Leander's advice?
dictates of divinity?
drops of lustral water in the sacrificial bowl?
bondage ancient in wrath
fatal vessel or net
leave your ancestral seat
o my general
& may commands be quick to get your release

barbarians had a hand in it
she is no longer a captive anima she is a subject of the state

you will remember we did things in our youth, Arjuna
won't compare you to blond Helen anymore I promise
the way she walks brazenly now as if two world wars
    hadn't taken many tolls is disturbing...

the neighborhood gets glitzy, pan-sexual
I've signed on

the hills you say?   going my way?

---

brunette
henna
silk or straw

wrist: pivots

hand: guide

knee: out of my way

Hand

wanton dominant mode never glitzy
mimicry of anatomy around girl-woman-love-talk
poem employs apostrophe
for solipsism on tender breast
will be screened

she is Parvati, Shakti, wife of Shiva
a gentle Durga and mother to Ganesh
her power floors you
in Ellora Cave, you weep reconsidering
the Kali Yuga if she were in charge

reanimate your voting record
narcissism is moot
in a passion of wild thought forms

the "other", remember, leaps
and you are the voyeur (*captive animal*)
and the preface world collapses in a flood

One is only New York or only Colorado
Only New Jersey or Nevada
or East Asia possibly, in a dream
but never insult the rock band you are the fan base of
reciprocity is a gypsy language
and you are votive to erotic mind

one of her pearls---"enough to buy and herd the finest goats in Broussa"

---

hand: *guide with a virtual string*
wrist: *pivots in writing this*
knee: *out of my way, children, and/or bend the generation*

Abdomen

ancestors go nameless til you ask
three thousand years in the floods
& bust a few pyramids
they're vagabonds too

stole the argument of asphodel
climbed Mt Athos, let my hair down
a stag no longer hiding behind a fig leaf

& see the thrush hop onto a branch
deer stepping shade to shade
insects again will buzz into the 21st and a half century

   away from Mars or be swallowed up?

in this document search a comet a commen a "connect"
such is the force of illusion waiting for the hurricane
in blind democracy

---

abdomen: *solid citizen*
stomach: *vulnerable on the Occupy! battlefield*
cheek: *a definition that raises itself and some be "cheeky"*

THUMBNAIL

feminine art controversy? do not spray
we're regressing here in the manner of social and civil rights

ostrasized, never
never go homeless into the void, fight back

deep in time things are done out of contrariness

cast away pretense, charm the winds of Thrace
speech! speech! before the angry mob
& a clamor for pride

dreamed in the Greek dream I gave birth to a snake
and had a laugh with the other damsels

wanted the ones who were feminists to cheer
but they didn't (did I?) get the joke

I was their school teacher……………………………………………..
………………………………………..[]
[]………………………………………………………..[].
pencil over my ear

---

thumbnail: *retrograde*
forearm: *necessary*
thumbprint: *obsolete*

LASH

"weibliche Arbeiten"
woman's work is never shunned

knuckles: rapt

the pudenda chronicles
look up to see the pillaging Zeus?

can you spin? will you be scanned?
are you mad?
groves & shrines, dance around my course description

"Madchen"
"jeunes filles"

what is the art of our love?

he went thinking, the shes kept circling the
liberated hearth, escaped into the streets

memory, meanwhile, kept steady
and standing on the soapbox heads turn

---

lash: *febrile*
nose: *in profile*
hairline: *reconstitute for the fabricant*

Corrêa: awake

Gaze: masked identity

Palm: extended

GAZE

syntactic weakness
fin de siècle decadence
I mean the last go-round

was she pure?

waiting for a future society to take over
hermeneutics for everyone……………..
lens of rescue

did we miss the absentee ballot procedure?
[ ] [ ]

Hetairia! my friends
welcome to the symposium
and sing all night because we are all suppliants here

she is not an island of paypals
where beauty is set apart and purchased
no!

———————————————————————

gaze: *masked identity*
palm: *extends*
cornea: *awake*

Wrinkles

come of repartee of wit of witless of witness
come of a dirty counterpane awake
how red the general's neck is
come home with me
[text goes silent here as if embarrassed]

[then resumes as if a cycle of a moon later]

come Andromeda

armada [again], come

lanterns as if moving away from cattle

are you a shell for adventure?

leave the raft, cut me adrift

come when you remember Constantinople

come a paper trail

come the trails of my tears

come swing states and help us out now

come to New York and trust your sanity

nothing is stricter than weather when it destroys

are we mere scrolls?

welcome to the symposium

---

wrinkles: *premonitions*

Tongue

in conclusion
we love in desperate times
we know too much. poetry adds it up

Pindar said "glossa"
and some compounds: straight-tongued, tongue-less

but never false. he said praise

poetry is an oral medium and has function in society and had to agree
you need a poet to speak for you

I set this down with a tireless voice out of heart-stopping fear
(*phonan akamatan*)

something like that and signed it:

"your scribe"

---

tongue: *thrust of the mentions of forehead*
throat: *the giver of life*
larynx: *starts with "hello, my laborious bellicose species"*

Fragments

In the *topos* in the products of human making in repositories in which they dwell in the body of sculpture, painting, amphora, lives Eros. Fraught or repressed. Figures chase each other around a vase or burn in Purgatorio on a George Schneeman vase. Perpetual hunt, things going after each other in the springtime, in battle time. Or Thanatos for a non-human, lives in a non-human variable. Lives inside an idea I will write to tell you the verbal attention of. Of the word presses, as "presses against my heart". Ideas press. Tell you what is seen in melancholia. It presses, the stylus, the stalk. It presses. O my world.

Rune and wreck. Symbols of themselves, What is seen in a subject transcending how you derogatorily say, "dwelling in primitive"—can you really spend your day looking, breathing in the "objects" of action to be crude? Be ritual. Be golden. Not action-bound entirely. But I do make. We do make. I do make up. We do make up. Make a case for this meaning in statue or poem, in painting or poem, a love affair or poem, biopic or poem, container for thoughts and fragments of one day—a line might be the mutilated body of the art you cherish. Paper we cherish. Bull-rushes. Let's go to surface. Artist eye please begging you rescue from mess and message. Lines are, conduits are, tributaries are, the trajectory-documents are constructions more than a statue or a poem collective is. All poems are fragments. That is a long ambulation. Around and around. What about the ordinary statute of things? Limitation. Composite miracles to cut up. When they rock and go brittle, when they refute entrance, when they excuse themselves from reproach, when they abjure taking a stance, when they seem to tame, reticent, murky, are they not fragments of ball-wreck impermanence? When murky becomes a problem for the historians of readers who examine "us" in distant future. *What was it to read? What was it to look? Who tamed the frame? What is it to mechanize?* What if your factotum does it for you? And reports back. You etch away in solid solitude. Museum shadow. Or. Or if. But two minds together is a boon, Will you be confused by the two variable, left brain and right? Can you be your own third mind? Are you lonely in all you do. I guess yes. Is your machine very murky, do you clear it every day. Don't be a fetishist. Don't reboot too often. Look at someone else's pictures. A collector of rare beings. And what is valuable are the feminized body parts that add up to a greater sum of extensions that ask the limits of the body as represented by deities, by goddesses, by sublimated animals, by helmeted warriors, by super-beings that wish to wink and smile as pure and salutary folly. At you. Female power and folly is the game of purveyors, of readers. Revelers. Revelators. I will go oral and demand attention. Drag this salutary transmission into public space. Sing my dithyramb. The page will be as bone, will be a steel trap, will be constructed of a substance hard to tamper with. Maybe the wood of forefathers and mothers, or stone carvers formerly painted and capture inner vibrant eye. Poly-chromed metabolism. Idea of bed linen or wrapping shrouds for viewing before the body hits the tomb, a single jewel in the crown, or bodhisattva demands release from her vow. Or if she could just be sure of the intangible. You can never demand more from a saint than intangibility. Fragment is always waiting to trip you up or startle. The first relation to this mind and "other" is the child's illusion. Is child's separation. Is the bent stick, diviner's wand, twig-inspired reprimand by the museum guard for yearning to cross the line, cross the boundary, just a closer look at you, become one with the object as it melts as an alloy. Its silver its tin it bronze and you get down for it, before substance. Holy stone. If marble was a district for punishment what would it be? It would be luxurious. Are you savage or poet? Are you wood. Or the enemy of wood? Please worship wood. Please worship ink. Please worship stone. How may you bring together the mutilated fragments of all you put an eye to, that you need to take care of how do they assist you in your scroll? In your scribe's assignment. How they talk back. And comrade for your vision. And weather the taut visual. Topology is rare and wonderful for all workers. And warm breath of pneumatology. Imagine. And that your breath could wreak havoc on the treasury of this influx, and what a dangerous artist will accomplish with line might continue. Be careful, tread lightly. Lift the brush high. What we hold in secular space, behind glass, relics of martyrs, telltale papyrus, gouache and pigment is happy in sacred space. Black and white solipsistic power. See it. Obeisance. Will one culture's ethos obscure another? Not here. Never in the heroics of kinetic aura and demand. A sweet voice.

Anne Waldman has been a prolific poet, editor, professor, performer, creating radical hybrid forms for the long poem, both serial and narrative, and engaged in "documentary poetics", fueling her ethos as a cultural activist. She is a frequent collaborator with visual artists including George Schneeman, Donna Dennis, Richard Tuttle and Pat Steir. She is the author of the magnum opus *The Iovis Trilogy: Colors in the Mechanism of Concealment,* a feminist "intervention" taking on war and patriarchy with a Buddhist edge, which won the PEN Center 2012 Award for Poetry. Her book *Gossamurmur*, 2013, is an allegorical adventure and plea for poetry's archive which "reanimates sentient beings". She helped found and directed The Poetry Project at St Mark's in the 1960-70s and went on to co-found The Jack Kerouac School of Disembodied Poetics at Naropa University with Allen Ginsberg, where she continues to curate the Summer Writing Program. Widely travelled and translated, she has worked most recently in China, Morocco, India and France. She is a recipient of the Shelley Memorial Award and a Guggenheim Fellowship for 2013-14. She also received the American Book Award for lifetime achievement from the Before Columbus Foundation in 2015.   www.annewaldman.org

Pamela Lawton has exhibited in galleries and museums both locally and internationally, including one-person exhibitions at the Galeria Nacional in San Jose, Costa Rica, The Conde Nast Building, NY, 180 Maiden Lane, NY, The Atrium Gallery, NY, and the Galeria Isabel Ignacio in Seville, Spain. Group exhibitions including her work have been featured in Pierogi Gallery, NYC, Sideshow Gallery, NYC, Tibor De Nagy Gallery, NYC, The Artists' Museum, Lodz, Poland, and the Emmanuel Heller Gallery, Tel Aviv. Lawton is currently an Artist-In-Residence (AIR) at Chashama, NYC, and has been an AIR at the World Trade Center through the Lower Manhattan Cultural Council. Collaborations with poets include *Sweet-voiced [mutilated] Papyrus*, Anne Waldman (Spyuyten Duyvil, 2015), *Walking After Midnight*, Bill Kushner (Spuyten Duyvil,2011), and A Place In the Sun (Spuyten Duyvil, 2010), Lewis Warsh. Interviews featuring her one-person exhibitions were featured on NY 1 News, in November 2011, and November 2009. She received a BA from Bennington College in visual arts and an MFA in painting from the City College in New York and Scuola Lorenzo De Medici in Florence, Italy. While a faculty member at New School University, she created a study-abroad art program in Sri Lanka. She has been teaching at the Metropolitan Museum of Art for more than ten years, and is on the faculty of Manhattanville College.

www.ingramcontent.com/pod-product-compliance
Lightning Source LLC
Chambersburg PA
CBHW051355110526
44592CB00024B/2991